W9-AAE-503

Police Cars

Quinn M. Arnold

CREATIVE EDUCATION • CREATIVE PAPERBACKS

seedlings

WOODRIDGE PUBLIC LIBRARY
3 PLAZA DRIVE
WOODRIDGE, IL 60517-5014
(630) 964-7899

Published by Creative Education and Creative Paperbacks
P.O. Box 227, Mankato, Minnesota 56002
Creative Education and Creative Paperbacks are imprints of
The Creative Company
www.thecreativecompany.us

Design by Ellen Huber; production by Dana Cheit
Art direction by Rita Marshall
Printed in the United States of America

Photographs by Alamy (Melvyn Longhurst, Alex Segre, Kumar
Sriskandan), Dreamstime (Frogtravel, Nerthuz, John Roman, Luis
Miguel Caselles San Segundo), Getty Images (Tom Hall/EyeEm),
iStockphoto (anouchka, Anton_Sokolov, CHUYN, csfotoimages,
DenisKot, infospeed, Jitalia17, kali9, mikeinlondon, no_limit_
pictures, Onfokus, wsfurlan)

Copyright © 2019 Creative Education, Creative Paperbacks
International copyright reserved in all countries. No part of
this book may be reproduced in any form without written
permission from the publisher.

Library of Congress Cataloging-in-Publication Data
Names: Arnold, Quinn M., author.
Title: Police cars / Quinn M. Arnold.
Series: Seedlings.
Includes bibliographical references and index.
Summary: A kindergarten-level introduction to police cars,
covering their purpose, parts, community role, and such
defining features as their flashing lights and sirens.
Identifiers: ISBN 978-1-64026-069-6 (hardcover) / ISBN 978-1-
62832-657-4 (pbk) / ISBN 978-1-64000-185-5 (eBook)

This title has been submitted for CIP processing under LCCN
2018939101.

CCSS: RI.K.1, 2, 3, 4, 5, 6, 7; RI.1.1, 2, 3, 4, 5, 6, 7; RF.K.1, 3; RF.1.1

First Edition HC 9 8 7 6 5 4 3 2 1
First Edition PBK 9 8 7 6 5 4 3 2 1

TABLE OF CONTENTS

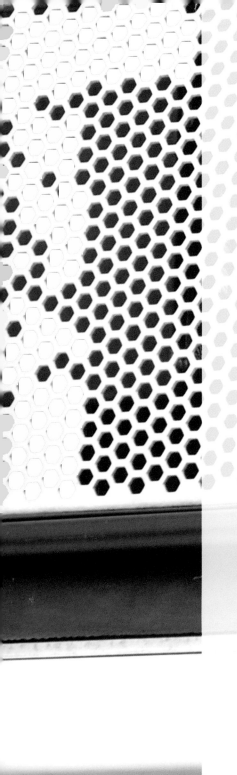

Hello, police cars!

Police cars patrol neighborhoods. They take police officers where they need to go.

They bring people to the police station.

Many police cars are black and white.

Others are blue, gray, tan, or dark red.

A police car has many lights that flash.

Eee-ooo-eee-ooo!
Its siren wails.

11

One police officer drives the car. Another officer may ride along.

They make sure people are being safe.

A police car has four tires. Sometimes it needs to get places quickly.

A powerful engine helps it go fast.

Police cars go on patrols. They stop to help people.

They keep communities safe.

Goodbye, police cars!

Picture a Police Car

light bar

mirror

battering ram

POLICE

POLICE DEPARTMENT CITY OF NEW YORK

NYP

HYBRID

headlight

tire

siren

www.nypdrecruit.com

RECRUIT 4330₁₃

COURTESY
PROFESSIONALISM
RESPECT

doors

taillight

engine: a machine that provides power and makes something move

patrol: keep watch over an area

siren: something that makes loud noises as a sign that an emergency vehicle is coming

Read More

Morey, Allan. *Police Cars*.
Minneapolis: Jump!, 2015.

Oachs, Emily Rose. *Police Cars*.
Minneapolis: Bellwether Media, 2017.

Websites

Police Car Coloring Pages
http://www.getcoloringpages.com/police-car-coloring-pages
Print out a picture of a police car to color.

YouTube: Heroes of the City – All About Police Cars
https://www.youtube.com/watch?v=a0If3uIGjEU
Watch a video to learn more about police cars and the equipment
they carry.

Note: Every effort has been made to ensure that the websites listed above are suitable for children, that they have educctional value, and that they contain no inappropriate material. However, because of the nature of the Internet, it is impossible to guarantee that these sites will remain active indefinitely or that their contents will not be altered.

Index